Miracle Fruit

miracle

fruit

poems by

Aimee Nezhukumatathil

TP

TUPELO PRESS
North Adams, Massachusetts

Tupelo Press

PO Box 1767, North Adams, Massachusetts 01247

413.664.9611 • Fax 413.664.9711

editor@tupelopress.org • web www.tupelopress.org

Cover and text designed by William Kuch, WK Graphic Design

If Heaven drops a date, open your mouth.

                              –Chinese proverb

for Paz del Fierro Celino Nezhukumatathil
and Mathew Joseph Nezhukumatathil

Contents

III Flesh

ONE BITE

Miracle fruit changes the tongue. One bite,
and for hours all you eat is sweet. Placed
alone on a saucer, it quivers like it's cold
from the ceramic, even in this Florida heat.

Small as a coffee bean, red as jam—
I can't believe. The man who sold
it to my father on Interstate 542 had one
tooth, one sandal, and called me

"Duttah, Duttah." I wanted to ask what
is that, but the red buds teased me
into our car and away from his fruit stand.
One bite. And if you eat it whole, it softens

and swells your teeth like a mouthful
of mallow. So how long before you lose
a sandal and still walk? How long
before you lose the sweetness?

I Slice

FISHBONE

At dinner, my mother says if one gets stuck
in your throat, roll some rice into a ball
and swallow it whole. She says things
like this and the next thing out of her mouth

is *did you know Madonna is pregnant?*
But I want to ponder the basket of fried smelt
on the table, lined with paper towels to catch
the grease—want to study their eyes

like flat soda, wonder how I'm supposed
to eat them whole. Wonder why we can't
have normal food for breakfast like at Sara's house—
Cheerios, or sometimes if her mother is home:

buttered toast and soft-boiled eggs
in her grandmother's dainty blue egg cups
and matching blue spoon. Safe. Pretty.
Nothing with eyes. Under the flakes of fried crust,

I see a shimmer of skin as silver as foil,
like the dimes my mother tapes to a board
for each year I'm alive. How she tucked this
into my suitcase before I left for college

and I forgot about '93 *and* '95. How she said
she'll never find a '93, and shouldn't this
be a great thing to one day put into an oak frame,
but not now, not until we find the missing coin?

How we don't have many traditions left, thanks
to Your Father. These are the things she says
instead of a blessing to our food. These are the words
that stick inside me as I snap off the next head.

STEALING SONG

"WELCOME TO THE PHILIPPINES,
THE ONLY CATHOLIC COUNTRY IN ASIA!
(beware of pickpockets)"
—billboard outside Metro Manila

We dupe you kindly:
>   an extra letter silk-screened
>   on stacks of T-shirts
in the *Los Santos* markets.
>   Or maybe in a fliver
>   of colored bills, a wave of hand
as we rush you through
>   the checkout line, sliding some
>   under the counter for later.
But we smile.
>   We smile always, talk clicks
>   and questions about the latest
American movie star, offer tips
>   on where to dine. I pray
>   you don't see my hand
in your shopping bag, tucking
>   that scarf for your sister—blue
>   as lobster blood—into my pocket.
The thrill of your bauble
>   in my palm is almost
>   like having pesos to buy it
myself. We mean no harm.
>   We will never split
>   your skin, not like ones
from the North. We sing
>   your safe travel, bags
>   a little lighter than before.
We wish you dreams
>   of sweet tomato and platters
>   of pig heads, mouths open,
saying *ah* and *oh*.

OOTY LAKE

"...where it is quite possible to arrange an elephant ride
and see many other wild animals."
—Guide for Traveling Abroad in India

The man yells *Audivaggani!* and smacks the beast's back leg. My saddle
is oily and fringed with tassel, all around us a gurgle of magpie, insect,
lake. Black monkeys zip through the elephant's legs as we rumble
ahead and I lean over to shoo them from their game. There sits a tiger
with toes spread into the shoreline, one tooth curling over his lip
like a joke no one forgets. In eighth grade, I asked a boy to dance
who said *I'm not feeling that wild right now* and would I consider
another? Another boy, another song? I did not ask; all night I sipped
cola with Sara and wondered when and where I'd find a wild one
who dances, who sings, who sees all the reds of a jungle.

WRAP

I don't mean when a movie ends,
as in, *it's a*! Nor tortillas splitting
with the heavy wet of bean.
And I don't mean what you do

with your lavender robe—all fluff
and socks—to snatch the paper
from the shrubs. Nor the promise
of a gift, the curl and furl of red ribbon

just begging to be tugged. What I mean
is waiting with my grandmama (a pause
in the Monsoon) at the Trivandrum airport
for a jeep. Her small hand wraps

again the emerald green pallu of her sari
tucked in at her hips, across her breast,
and coughs it up over her shoulder—a hush
of paprika and burnt honey across my face.

TABLE MANNERS

In India, Northerners pride themselves
on eating only with their fingertips,
while Southerners enjoy their foods
with the entire hand, to the wrist if need be.

No wonder JoAnn and I sit stunned
at the dinner table as our cousins
scoop and slurp their lunch: dried fish
in gingilly oil, poori soaked first

in sambar then cooled in cucumber rayta.
I motion to Oomana, the servant girl:
do you have fork, spoon? She laughs
a little longer than necessary, then

disappears into the storage room.
Each finger-lick makes us grimace
but secretly I want to join them
in slick-smacking this beautiful food.

The three-year old sees my fork
and cries until he gets one
of his own to bang and draw
lines in his plate of sauce.

No one here ever wishes
you happiness and now I know why:
this is supposed to be of your own doing,
your own relish, of your own open hands.

PEACOCKS

At Chowpatty Beach, people strip
only from the ankles down. Yogis

bury themselves up to the neck
in sand, each turban tagged

with a single blue medallion. I watch
as a little boy offers a violet guava—

the yogi turns away, doesn't blink. Here,
everyone looks only into my eyes; not once

do I catch anyone glance at my bare leg.
My neighbor back in Ohio kept

a peacock tied to her sycamore tree.
By winter, the rope shredded

and the peacock walked the stiff grass
freely, a scarf around its neck.

I wanted to steal a feather
and tape it to my jeans. How

a simple turn of head makes
all the difference. All those eyes.

AANABHRANDHANMAR MEANS 'MAD ABOUT ELEPHANTS'

Forget trying to pronounce it. What matters
is that in southern India, thousands are afflicted.
And who wouldn't be? Children play with them
in courtyards, slap their gray skin with cupfuls
of water, shoo flies with paper pompoms.
When the head of the household leaves

for business, his elephant weeps fat tears
of joy when he returns. Their baths of husk
and stone last four hours, every wrinkle
rubbed and patted with cinnamon oil.
At festival, silk caps and gold tassels drape
their broad heads. Brides still wear

rings of its stiff tail hair, part of their dowry
to avoid evil eye. A man with blue sandals
told me that elephants are cousins to the clouds—
that they belonged to Lord Indra, king
of the gods, that elephants were his carriage
in the wind—that they once had wings.

GULABJAMOON JAR

I love saying the name. Each sweet syllable seems like there ought to be a crush of sugar on your tongue, a tiny reward just for saying the word. These soft milk-balls, fried golden and soaked in sugar syrup, are glassed up in a luxuriously oversized jar that my grandmother collects under her spice table to store homemade mango and spicy lime pickles. But for Uncle Jacob, these jars serve as seasonal aquariums. When I asked him where the fish in the gulabjamoon jar (now sitting in the center of his dining table) came from, he said *after rain, these fish appear in road puddles*. Uncle asked a boy to catch some in a towel: a present for my aunt. These fish are small, two inches long. A black teardrop shape behind each eye, and again, if you didn't catch it the first time, on the tail. Odd because they don't have the traditional fish 'shape,' where the body tapers into a kissy mouth and ends in a swish of tail—more like little silver rectangles suspended in the jar. Uncle said when the puddles dry up in the sun, the fish aren't there to crack and split their smooth milkskins. He's never yet seen one dead in the street. Like the fish knew they had to move to a new wet place. Perhaps they were snatched up by a dog or pecked to bits by a rooster. All over the village, wet dogs and wet chickens roam the moss-covered alleys. Nobody knows who cares for these animals but all of them have a crafty gleam in their eye that says: *Yes, I ate more than even you today*. On the table, the fish watch me watch them eat rice, the only food my aunt gives them. I see the rice fluff in their bellies, swelling. I tap the jar with a fork and the only response is a slight shift in their togetherness—a white square of silk thrown into a small sea.

THE ROLLING SAINT

> Lotan Baba, a holy man from India, rolled on his side for
> four thousand kilometers across the country in his quest for
> world peace and eternal salvation.
>
> *—Reuters*

He started small: fasting here and there,
days, then weeks. Once, he stood under
a banyan tree for a full seven years, sitting
    for nothing—not even to sleep. It came
    to him in a dream: *You must roll*
    on this earth, spin your heart in rain,
        desert, dust. At sunrise he'd stretch, swab
        any cuts from the day before, and lay prone
        on the road while his twelve men swept
the ground in front of him with sisal brooms.
Even monkeys stopped and stared at this man
rolling through puddles, past storefronts
where children would throw him pieces
of butter candy he'd try and catch
in his mouth at each rotation. His men
    swept and sang, swept and sang
    of jasmine-throated angels
    and pineapple slices in kulfi cream.
        He rolled and rolled. Sometimes
        in his dizzying spins, he thought
        he heard God. A whisper, but still.

SWEAR WORDS

Even now I laugh when I see the look on my mother's face
when I swear in Tagalog. I have no idea what these phrases
really mean, but they've been spattered on me since I was still
a fat, bawling baby—and scattered onto my head when I've toppled

juice glasses on white carpet or come home past curfew.
Sometimes even the length of my skirts or driving her through
a red light produces ones with a bit of a gasp, a wet sigh
of disapproval. Now I catch myself saying them out loud

when I knock my knee against the coffee table,
slice a bit of my knuckle with paper. When I asked her,
she told me one phrase meant 'God,' so of course I feel guilty.
Another is 'crazy female lost piglet,' which doesn't even

make sense when I think of the times I've heard her use that,
and still others, she claims, are untranslatable. But the one
I love best is *Diablo*—devil—pronounced: *Jah-blew!* She uses it
as if to tell me, "I give up! You do what you want but don't

come running to me," after I tell her I bounced a check
or messed up a romance with a boy she finally approved of.
Diablo! Diablo! Here comes a little red devil, tiny pitchfork
in hand, running past the terra-cotta flower pots

in my mother's sunroom *Diablo! Diablo!* And still another from behind
the kitchen curtains, a bit damp from the day's splashes of the sink.
Today when they meet, they dance a silly jig on the countertop, knock
over the canister of flour, leave little footprints all over the place.

HELL PIG

To keep me from staying out late at night,
my mother warned of the *Hell Pig*. Black and full

of hot drool, eyes the color of a lung—it'd follow me
home if I stayed past my curfew. How to tell my friends

to press *Pause* in the middle of a video, say their good-byes
while I shuffled up the stairs and into my father's waiting

blue car? How to explain this to my dates, whisper
why we could not finish this dance? It's not like the pig

had any special powers or could take a tiny bite
from my leg—only assurances that it was simply

scandal to be followed home. When my date and I
pull into my driveway and dim the lights, we take

care to make all the small noises that get made
in times like these even smaller: squeaks in the seats,

a slow spin of the radio dial, the silver click of my belt.
Too late. A single black hair flickers awake the ear

of the dark animal waiting for me at the end of the walk.
My fumbling of keys and various straps a wild dance

to the door—the pig grunting in tune to each hurried step, each
of his wet breaths puffing into tiny clouds, a small storm brewing.

THE PURCHASE

After I finish explaining to my mother
that my boyfriend and I just bought a puppy,
she tells me the story of a family she knew
in the Philippine village where she grew up:
how the family left their baby in the house
with the dog while they went to market. How
they returned—bags full of chico fruits, ube roots,
and mango—to find the dog outside, mouth
bloody and excited. How the father hacked
the matted dog to bits while the mother ran
inside expecting to find the infant's remains,
but all that was left was a dead snake
near the crib and their fat baby
happy and giggling. And then she says nothing.

    And I say nothing, this is how we talk: stories

instead of opinions in the here and now. What
comes next I could have guessed—the one about
her famously numerous suitors, the stories that make
my father sigh and pretend to be engrossed
in his paper. The one about the engineer
who showed up at her door in Chicago with a dachshund
under his arm. How she fed the dog sausages and cheese
and later forgot it in a park, like a glove or knit hat—
she was so mad it didn't find its way home! And there's
nothing more I can tell her: nothing about choosing
a teeny collar, a name, watching your love fold
old blankets into a crate. The surprising star-shaped paw prints
near the water dish. She will remember only the dangers, the blood,
her one attempt lost near the rose gardens and hysterical geese.

TELLING THE BEES

"Little bee your master is dead.
Leave me not in my necessity."
–German folksong

The man wearing a hive-shaped hat complete with little nylon bees
dangling from the sides of his head sees me holding a waxy bottle
of honey and asks, Do you know how to talk to bees?
I'm not sure if this is a pick-up line and suddenly I notice
we're the only ones in the entire produce department. I step back
prepare to head somewhere safer, like the bakery,
but he goes on about how the secret way to prevent stings
is to talk to them first if you decide to move their hive.

I'm thinking, What could possibly possess me
to pick up a hive on my own? When I was little
I was scared of men at carnivals who covered
their whole chest and neck with them—a bee shirt.
But this man says *a hive must be kept aware of all*
the happenings in a house. Leave the bees a crumb
of wedding or funeral cake. Let them know
they're still part of the family.

I need to get back to selecting a bouquet
of broccoli, some red potatoes, but I don't leave.
When this strange man asks if I know anything
about bees—anything at all—*I* tell him my favorite
is the bumble, their fat bottoms bouncing
along a fence of cornflowers; the first bees
came from Christ's tears on the cross; at midnight
on Christmas Eve, you can hear whole hives singing

Psalm 100: *Come before Him, Come before Him...*
I don't like the idea of any animal singing,
and at night to boot. But now I'm drawn
to that quiet hum, the notion that a whole colony
could stop its business for one small moment
and shake out a hymn on legs and wing as thin
as a baby's eyelash. Who can say it's not true, the song
silver in the ears of those who choose to listen?

FALLING THIRDS

We measure our names the same.
Across the world, when children
call out for a friend, their mother,

their favorite white goat—they have
the same intonation, the same fall
and lilt to their voice, no matter

their language: *Jahhn-ee! Mah-ma!*
Pehh-dro! My music teacher friend says
this is *falling thirds*: this is proof we spoke

the same language before Babel, that maybe
a tower did fall into rock and dust, gilding
our tongues slicker past any understanding.

We speak little wants, call little kisses
into our ears across beanfields, sand,
saltwater. Still, we sing the same songs.

II Juice

SUDDENLY AS ANYTHING

with thanks to Jennifer Vanderbes

One of my students uses this to describe
the way a person leaves the room and I circle
it with a question mark, scribble: *Too Vague*
with my red pen. During my snowy walk home,

I bury my nose into my already damp scarf, wonder
if I'm a bad teacher, how this student could possibly
miss the whole point of my metaphor lecture
and if this ice won't give just a little bit for my boots.

But the more I think about it, I think: *Genius!*
For who hasn't vanished without so much as a trace
of waxy lip prints on a glass, not even leaving
a single stray hair on the back of a chair? Sometimes

disappear means *leave quickly so I don't feel your absence.*
Carpenter ants don't even shake one last message
to their beloved queen before they crawl
into a smooth piece of driftwood and set sail

for new shores. When he drove away last winter,
I avoided looking at the ground for days so I would not
find an imprint of his shoe. And maybe what my student
meant was *anything* can be loss, even the good things:

a ring juicy with rubies, a new spaniel pup, an orange
so fat its segments beg to be unfolded like a blossom
in your hand. Even when the chara plant, the world's
first known underwater vegetation, suddenly

disappeared, it gave no warning—never even feigned
a withering of its bubbly leaves, its hardy stems
curling in and around bedrock, brushing the scales
of mysterious striped fish until its very last day.

IN PRAISE OF COLOPHONS

Just when I think I'm finished reading my book,
I turn the last page and find that the lettering
of this softened paperback was first cut
by a monk in 1739, just off the Northern coast
of France. How delightful, this production
by the sea—no talking, only the small splashes
of wave against rock, a plover's squawk,
the metal plink of each letter into the carriage.

Another book states that in spite of the youthful age
of *Berling Roman's* typeface, it carries an old face's
personality: the serifs thick and blunt, inclined,
and most importantly, the g has a straight ear.
How I'd love to pinch its bulbous nose! The tufts
of silver silk hair like a low crown around its head!

My favorite colophon reports that another monk
designed *Carlyle* over two centuries ago. Its letters
sit round and open as fishbowls on a windowsill.
The balance so delicate, one strong wind
could spill the glass and its slippery contents
across the stone floor. O, but the light in each
watery leaf, the small transparencies in those fins—
the arc of orange fish that leap and leap and leap.

WINTER GAMES

On their January honeymoon, Edison and wife experimented with electrocuting oysters. Someone stole all three oranges—pendulant, still tinged green—from my mother's backyard. She made a sign out of an old box flap that said, "WHO STOLE IT?" carefully lettered in black ball-point, tied it with green thread into the branches of her tree. My dog is a blue snowplow in front of me searching for wet unmentionables in plastic bags left over from Fall. I have no idea who stuffed a riot of pine cones and holly in my mailbox. All over the beach, hundreds of oysters bubble their last breath, shells blown wide open.

THE WOMAN WHO TURNED DOWN
A DATE WITH A CHERRY FARMER
Fredonia, NY

Of course I regret it. I mean there I was under umbrellas of fruit
so red they *had* to be borne of Summer, and no other season.
Flip-flops and fishhooks. Ice cubes made of lemonade and sprigs
of mint to slip in blue glasses of tea. I was dusty, my ponytail
all askew and the tips of my fingers ran, of course, *red*

from the fruitwounds of cherries I plunked into my bucket
and still—he must have seen some small bit of loveliness
in walking his orchard with me. He pointed out which trees
were sweetest, which ones bore double seeds—puffing out
the flesh and oh the surprise on your tongue with two tiny stones

(a twin spit), making a small gun of your mouth. Did I mention
my favorite color is red? His jeans were worn and twisty
around the tops of his boot; his hands thick but careful,
nimble enough to pull fruit from his trees without tearing
the thin skin; the cherry dust and fingerprints on his eyeglasses.

I just know when he stuffed his hands in his pockets, said
Okay. Couldn't hurt to try? and shuffled back to his roadside stand
to arrange his jelly jars and stacks of buckets, I had made
a terrible mistake. I just know my summer would've been
full of pies, tartlets, turnovers—so much jubilee.

FRUIT COCKTAIL TREE

According to my Michigan Bulb Company catalog,
this tree will produce *tasty peaches, juicy nectarines,*
tangy apricots, and plump purple plums. I'm all ready
to order this amazing plant—*guaranteed* to grow

it says—but I have to wonder why the only picture
available is an artist's rendering—no clear crisp
photo like the ones for Pink Cosmos
or Mosquito Plant. The Cinnamon Fern looks

so robust so fiery it could burst into flame
right there on the page. Tiptoeing across
a lawn's border, Peacock Orchids are a bit shy
but the brilliant blue (*blue!*) just kills me.

What you'll really get if you order the Fruit Cocktail Tree
is anybody's guess. In the drawing, there is a lady
in jaunty slacks and wispy blouse reaching high
above her head to pluck a purple fruit, of which I count

at least forty others. The rest of the colorful spheres
look suspiciously alike, all the same rusty shade
of orange as if stenciled by some sweaty guy
in the back of a studio with a box labeled "CIRCLES."

I wonder if the woman in the drawing is his girlfriend
or just someone in his art class he secretly
adores. The wicker basket she holds is so full
she couldn't possibly eat them all. Perhaps he hopes

she will ask him to share this fruit with a plate
of cubed cheese, checked cloth, ice water. They won't
even notice the ants coming closer, closer—waving
their antennae as if conducting a symphony.

IN THE POTATOES

Early Scots refused to eat (it was not
mentioned in the Bible): leprosy, blindness—
its supposed costly price. *"One potato,
two potato, three potato, four!"*
Misunderstood too: Captain Cook,
Walter Raleigh, even Catherine the Great

tried to convince people of the glorious crop
but failed. Lord Byron lamented its aphrodisiac effects
...'Tis after all a sad result of passions and potatoes.
The Quencha Indians of Peru have over one thousand
words for this crop. They dance a two-step during harvest,
pant legs rolled to knees, every jump a push of water

from the bitter, marble-sized tubers to make *chuno* paste.
In the blackfrost night, it dries, feeds a whole village
for two seasons: crystal starch. Potato spirits
made of rock line up in threes, hum soil-songs
through rooftops into ears of sleeping infants.
Estar en las papas—to be in the potatoes—

means a person has finally risen to afford more
than a banana diet. In the Paucartambo Valley
of Peru, I read the soft earth like Braille, gather
some on my own, each hardness a possibility.
Tiny pineapples, coral snakes, purple gumdrops—
anything but the brown oval spud I know. A small, flat one:

mishipasinghan—means cat's nose; a knobby,
difficult-to-peel kind is *lumchipamundana*—or, *potato
makes young bride weep.* The Acumbo village
sees a surplus of this kind in late summer.
Housewives grind their teeth with each peel,
stifle shivers into aprons, curse the abundant fruit.

CONFUSIONS

Honeybees hum the correct curtsy
to their queen, smudge pollen
in the right waxy cell. Roaches
the size of a baby's sweet shoe
die every day but where exactly
are they disposed of? Do I write his silence,
the pulse and flex in his face as we sit
in his Pontiac, his blue breath wetting
the wheel? Year after year, lacy patterns
of star pull birds back South where I look out
over a veranda, count the crashes of water
and rock. I've noticed he's changed
his handwriting—now it's all squares and shelves—
small, burnt cakes on a plate, even his O's.

LEWIS AND CLARK DISAGREE

Because Merriwether ate the last berry
without consulting William. Because

the prairie dog only let *William* feed
it dried corn. Because the Nez Perce

gave one a necklace of purple quartz
and not the other. Because osage oranges

gave Merriwether hives. Because a grizzly
chased William into an oak tree, left him

high for hours. Because "Someone" tucked
buffalo chips into Merriwether's knapsack

when he wasn't looking. Because after walking,
rowing, swimming, climbing, trotting, pulling,

cutting, all they really wanted was a name
for a fruit one found sour, the other, so sweet.

CHEESE CURDS, THE FIRST TIME

Dairy aisle, and I'm confused. No one explains
why here in southern Wisconsin, all I can find
in the chilled silver bins at my local grocery
are blocks of orange 'cheese food,' wheels of it,
even *sliced*, individually wrapped if I desire.
Of course it's food, but the fact they

have to qualify it makes me suspicious.
And rightly so, says my neighbor, leaning
a meaty elbow out her window. In between
bites of potato salad she says, *You's gotta go*
to the Farmer's Market and getchu some
cheeeese curds. The way yellow oozes
out of the corners of her mouth when she says

this makes it hard to even sip my cola later
as I wander the maze of fresh produce and people
in wide-brimmed hats. A swarm descends on a booth
selling said curds, each person wanting the freshest bag-full:
white chunks, bite-sized, more solid than I imagined,
just a bit salty *and* sweet. Even a baby's
pink, fat hand (hoisted high above us) clamors

for a waxy bag of her very own. How I love
the grab and pull for something you can't name, only
knowing you want more. The thinness in your voice
as you try to describe all the breads and heaps
of fresh beans just waiting to be snapped.
I have not yet mentioned the squeak in your teeth.

WHY I AM NOT AFRAID OF KING COBRAS
Kerala, India

Forests equal fairies for a girl of eight.
What I did not equate was this was *jungle*,
just off the edge of coconut groves
and rubber trees, land where even my father

never ventured alone as a boy. But this
was vacation, time off from spelling tests
and fractions. All of a sudden I had grandparents
to buy me pieces of pink candy, and glass bangles

that clinked with each swing of arm. After dinner, I loved
to gouge the rubber trees with a stick, watch the plastic
ooze from each gash, roll the warm sap into a ball—
each bounce so high, I'd lose them in the last flicks

of sun. I had wandered further that day, deeper
in the groves where cinnamon and sweetleaf grew like weeds.
When I reached for a new stick, I saw him there, standing
in what I learned later is the *Imperial* pose—eye level,

his teeny tongue tasting the air for what I smelled of:
candy and glass. The ribs of his neck spread wide
as my father's hand, then smoothed down, and I laughed—
he was suddenly small and naked, like he'd lost

his hat. We stood there for some time before I turned around
and went back inside to tell no one that just minutes before,
a girl and snake made their introductions—the birds overhead
holding their breath, the pierced trees bubbling at their bark.

I COME BACK TO GREEN

when I return from Palm Springs,
& all the grass is charged
with it, every blade brushed.
Cells square & light.
The dark center
like a single grape, pulsing
with sun. Rye seeds plucked
one by one to find who
I will marry: *tinker, tailor,*
soldier, sailor, rich man, poor man,
beggar man, thief. I want to end
on the thief. Why is it when
the post office issues
green stamps, some national
catastrophe happens?
      Plane crash bearing
schoolchildren. Dogs stranded
on flooded rooftops biting
their own tails, little crescents
of fur & fear. You can get arrested
in Toledo, Ohio if you throw
a snake at someone. Even if it's
just a garter. Do the police stations
there have a desk for the crime?
& what kind of person works it—
someone who lunches too long,
slides into an already full elevator
just to get to the second floor.
I come back to green & realize
everyone is a suspect. Ferns unroll
with envy at the S flying in the air.
& the snake—for one brief moment—
knows what it's like to have wings.

THE ALLIGATOR

On the boat dock, I dangle and flit
my legs, the chew of wood etching
just below my cut-offs—two brown

birds dancing inches from the surface
of Lake Conine. A rotted snag of tree
washes near in this bay breeze—I read,

dip my hand in a ceramic cup of cherries,
spit the seeds (they totter down in small
splashes) at carefree intervals between

the point and lean of the sundial's
shadows. A closer look shows
a pair of night eyes steady,

holding fast in the current. I yike up my legs;
it glides past, I throw a cherry at the bulge
in the water but miss—my insult not even

blink-worthy to the creature.
The eyes pause for a moment in front
of the shore's cattails, dip below, pierce

the watery plain—and I am left
stretching to see where they
will resurface. A split of waterplants

proves its presence and its rest:
on the plush of fen mud,
its ancient smile as if it swallowed

a delicious secret a hundred
years ago and divulges it
only today, only for me.

CROW JOY

Almost all of the gold leaf on the Kremlin domes was scratched off years ago from the fleet of crows converging at the top. Contrary to popular belief, they were not stealing the shiny flakes for their nests, as they would a lovely kerchief pinned too loose on a clothesline, or withered breadfruit left too long in sun. A closer look revealed their game of sliding down those onion domes, their claws scraping the roofskin raw. In sunlight, crow wings flash a wild blue, as blue as the nose of a jolly mandrill. Half a world away, a family of these monkeys dips their fingers into a stream for the first time—their black fingernails dulled square for scratching stems to drink, their noses wet, warm. A shopkeeper near the *Lobnoye Mesto*, The Place of Skulls, once recorded distressed crow calls to scare the birds from their play. But the top was too high or the tape too quiet— the birds' feet already too gilded to ever want to step foot on this earth again.

THE WOMAN WHO HATES FROGS

In a teen club's sweet, secret pact
gone wrong, the girl was left
in a closet to hold whatever
was placed in her hand, no matter

what. *Survive this, and be one of us!*
Frog slipped from hand, hand to shoulder,
shoulder to floor. The spike of her heeled shoe
pierced the frog's slick back through to its belly,

spattered her bare calf. Thirty years later,
the woman who now hates frogs sips
juice from a blue glass in her screened-in
patio. She contemplates the hibiscus,

the patio thermometer that rises
with each thinning shadow in the yard,
flaps sandal against heel. Her daughters
know well her fear, guide her path

in pet and bookstores. In the back yard,
her garden creaks alive with dewy life
before the June sun reaches its highest
point. A frog's eye can be yellow,

red, a liquid gray. To a frog, a tiny, dark
matter is meaningful, particularly if it moves:
fibers in the eye send signals to snap
its tongue. After a long rain, the woman

sends her husband with an empty
jelly jar to the garden—a cruel harvest
so she may work the soil freely. Makes him
promise to tighten the lid, take its air quickly.

NEST SHIRT

University of Wisconsin Art Gallery, May 2001

On this collage, bird nests grow thick
& braided in the belly of a shirt.
A camisole—sheer white, but a little frayed

at the neck, as if some sparrow sisters
tried to pluck bits of its shiny thread
to line the cup of their home.

Small copper stamps that spell "OH,"
float above the shirt, sprinkled like
a metallic rain in the last salt of summer.

Do they stand for Ohio, the flat spaces
of green & green, the icy creeks
where I used to catch water bugs

in a red plastic cup? The city nights
of metal & festival, the "Oh!" from
the lips of boys & girls just before

roller coasters dip into that first
sweet plunge of the season. Simply
saying *oh*! makes a circle of your mouth,

teeth wet with possibility, a roundness
like that nest pitching itself home
on this shirt. Rub my belly. Feel the itch.

$2^{13,466,917} - 1$

Men with glasses at metal desks, rejoice:
the world's largest prime number. Found
by a twenty-year old. These four million,

fifty three thousand, nine hundred
and forty-six digits would take three
whole weeks to write out longhand.

No bathroom breaks. No sleep. Mersenne,
a French monk of math, boldly predicted
this precision over three hundred years ago,

but people called him crazy, made him go back
to his lily garden, his tiny marble fountain
with a dogface spout. The Fundamental Theory

of Arithmetic says prime numbers develop
unbreakable codes, message encryption, that they're
the building blocks of numbers. My little neighbor

swipes his building blocks across his gummy mouth,
can't yet read the A, the B, never mind the C. I try
arranging them to form words. He claps his hands

at the small stack in front of him and throws one
across the carpet, its pile already coming loose
from our socks, fingers—the millions and millions

of fibers springing free—just waiting, waiting for this.

CANTICLE WITH SEA WORM
for Doris Lohre

Blessed be the curly-haired lady at Penn Station
who directed me to my train in a sea of angry

trenched coats. Blessed be Brazilian hatchet fish
that leap the lake together for a snack of gnats.

Blessed be juice and raspberry vodka.
Blessed be the first day of the year for sandals.

Blessed be driftwood with mysterious eggs
inside. Blessed be Tess, the 50ft. Woman

with Visible Organs standing outside of Los Angeles.
I pulled over because of her neon sign,

the postcards, the t-shirt possibilities—
& had the cup of coffee that kept me driving

in between the lines. Blessed be the eunicids,
the tiny sea worms mouthing on bits of sand

& shell thanklessly at night, spitting up whole
platforms for the Great Barrier Reef to spread.

Blessed be any mother with cancer spots
on an otherwise perfectly milky x-ray. Ghost

of a heart large & light, just a trace of her supple arms,
a wedding ring. The silence of her children studying

the delicacy of a new fern, the crispy gift-foil around
each potted plant. The silence of waiting by her bed.

MEDITATION ON FLANNEL

I love the   sound.
          Push the *l*
with your tongue
to the back of your teeth.
Push again
at the end.
          Usually plaid.

Why? There's an   air   of formality

to it—deceives you when you press
          your cheek to plushy cloth:
the skin of an apricot.

Spread a sheet   of it and lie.
January chill is your mischievous doorman.

Cold/hot, then   warm/cool—don't worry: this material

will take care of you. Curl, suspire—dream
          of a basket lined with it,   full of   persimmons.
Sleep soft.

MAKING GYOTAKU

In Osaka, fishermen have no use for the brag,
the frantic gestures of length, blocks of air

between their hands. They flatten their catch
halfway into a tray of sand, steady

the slick prize. The nervous quiver
of the artist's hands over the fish—washing it

with dark ink, careful not to spill or waste,
else feel the wrath of salty men long at sea.

If it is a good print, the curves and channels of each scale
will appear as tidy patterns to be framed and hung

in the hallway of his house. But perhaps the gesture
I love most—before the pressing of rice paper over

inked fish, before the gentle peel away of the print
to show the fish's true size—is the quick-light stroke

of the artist's thumb, how deftly he wipes away
the bit of black ink from the fish's jelly eye—

how he lets it look back from the wall at the villagers,
the amazed staring back at the amazed.

THE BONSAI MASTER'S DAUGHTER BREAKS HER SILENCE

Let me say it was not easy
to listen to all the snips like tiny birds
chirping under the floorboards to my father's studio
downstairs. Those years of groaning branches wired
and tugged into a cascade, spilling over the base of the pot—
like mountain stream, like light. Most of all,
I hate the slants. Why these plum trees always sit
off-center, asymmetrical and empty in the place
where heaven meets earth in a ceramic pot.
What waste of air,
thick with the scent
of snipped fruit buds
and metal. I could
grow good there,
pale roots
whirling like a thumbprint
on his wrist. Some nights when I knew
he would be home late, I'd sneak into his room,
search the shapes of apricot and maple trees
for dragons, tigers, birds with wild tails.
Nothing like a girl
and her outstretched arm
scattering
food to fat
white fish.
Or a girl parting curtains, waving good-bye to her mother.
Sometimes he'd surprise me with *bon-kei:* small buildings
and people nestled right there in the black dirt, the trees
looming large in the center of the miniature city. A
tiny paper house could look alive with just
the light from a single match.

ARACHNE

The sweetest medium
is water. I envy the frog;
her mate holds her firm
in a wet embrace, then
the release—an egg froth
on her back and good-bye.
I cannot imagine a hunger
filled, a calm stretch of nerve.

My legs won't even break
the surface to let me dip
my body in. Perhaps a breeze,
perhaps a dew will come
to envelop me. In the branches
of this gum tree, I sigh. This air
is no good. Who knows
what god I will inhale.

LITTLE HOUSES

after Kenneth Koch

1

Frieda Kahlo lived
In a little house
With two mangy
Cats circling
Her garden for
Hummingbirds
She went out
And got hit
By a streetcar
Which twisted
Her back She had
To stay in bed
Most of the time
Even to paint
She married
Diego and at first
She painted
Happy scenes
Happy colors
But still he slept
With other women
And Frieda
Stayed in
Her paintings
Sad lots of blood
Tears and bodies like
A Few Small Nips
Which was actually
Plenty of nips
A sort of jest
She said, "I am
So often alone.
I am the subject
I know best."

2

Marie Antoinette lived
In a little house
She wore wigs
With feathers
And wigs with tiny
Wooden cakes
She loved
Cake she loved
To eat
That is all
They did in court:
Eat and wear wigs
She went out and
Spun the moon
Into her food
Louis did not care
Before they cut
Into Marie's neck
Her advisors asked
What they should do
About the little
People fighting
In the streets She said,
"Let them eat cake!"
Kept ordering
Her cooks to bake.

3

Harriet Tubman lived
In a little house
Had strong and fierce
Eyes She went out
And could see
In the night She
Carried a gun
And told her
Underground

Passengers She'd use
It on *them* if
They got fright
Had a husband John
Who left her
When She was Free
But she loved him
Even kept his name
Before bed he
Used to gently
Press his thumb
On Her forehead
Scars and smile
So when he left
To touch her
There
Was not allowed
Whenever Harriet
Crossed into freesoil
She said, "I's sure
Livin' In Heaven now."

III Flesh

SPEAK

If the Hopi say "ripi"
to mean *notch*, then
for them, *serration*
is "ripiripiripi." I want
to speak like that, fill
your ears and hands
with wet stones, turquoise
and smooth, as if
they had tumbled
in the mouth of a macaw.

COCOA BEACH, OFF-SEASON

Where sanderlings race to pluck
coquina clams from the sand,
jelly tongues still slapping for wet air.
A place where tourist-trap signs pluralize
things that shouldn't be: *hand-dipped ice creams,
fantastic surfs*. A family umbrellas a picnic
of egg salad sandwiches, canned cola
wrapped in foil, a bag of cherries—
and no one with gaudy gold bangles
or hat brims wide as a pelican's wing
will ever ask them to Move please,
you're blocking my sun. Two sisters
pack together sand and foam to make
igloos around their feet. A father jumps
the waves or talks to the local shellbacks
about what they have and haven't caught.
If you're lucky, you'll spy a ghost crab—
how he stands on claw tips, kicking
at his own door in the sand, how he cuts
the sand sideways to a tossed piece of bread.
Best of all are the small impressions
of a mother's feet into a shoreline
soft and dark as unfrosted cake. The prints
say, *Here* is where she lingered over
a Queen Conch shell. Here is where
she stayed the morning to gather bits:
fire sponges, jingle shells, a remnant of whelk.

LAGOON

As in Blue. As in wild. As in the salty space
where dozens of stingrays gather for a bit
of squid and crushed shrimp. Each animal
wider than my outstretched arms, wings

softer than I imagined, like a giant earlobe skimming
my calf. My sister and I tried to take pictures
of each other with a ray suspended
in the background—wore our brightest suits:

citrus tanks and red T-backs, the water clear
as gin—to no avail. Back in Ohio, we sighed
and grumbled at their absence in all the glossy photos
we sorted through. Here's one of JoAnn waving

with a tiny, yellow porkfish in the corner. See
the small squiggle on the left? That's me
and a seahorse. Another with her and a school
of blue tangs, but no stingrays, not even

one of their violet shadows on the ocean floor.
Now I think all the empty ocean and coral beds
behind us mean more, mean *Use Your Imagination*.
Can't you just picture the swoop of a dark pair

of wings beneath your flippered feet, the surprising
golden iris of their eyes like teeny underwater lights,
the ripple of a cold body burying itself in pink sand?
Yesterday, I called JoAnn and reached

her answering machine. I was startled by the voice—
like listening to my own—saying *I'm not here, please
leave a message*. I still have some pictures
from the Bahamas around my apartment,

love it when people mistake her for me. That
her frantic pointings to a spot outside the picture frame
are really mine too. That there is a voice five states away
that will always echo mine. That the bubbles of speech

she once gurgled to me underwater are still bouncing
off the sleek backs of all those astonishing stingrays.

COCO CAY

At Coco Cay, I snorkel
          close to the buoys
                    that mark where They
          are not responsible for you
anymore & find myself
          in a school of blue & gold
                    skipjack fish. Nothing but
          luminous fishcolor, small bits
of ocean. The skipjacks
          surround me, don't budge
                    unless I kick flippers. Would
          they be brave enough
to kiss me (they are known
          as kissing fish, pressing
                    their swollen blue lips
          to each other, a wall
of clams, aquarium glass)?
          A kite-shaped shadow
                    flies into focus a couple
          of yards away. Easy
to recognize the ray's slide,
          the undulation of wing
                    over a helpless line
          of shrimp. Panic. I flipper
my way back till I'm within
          shouting distance of shore.
                    Tiny red seahorses glide in
          & out of the coral shrubs.
I want one to curl
          its ribbed tail around
                    my finger, a mermaid's ring.
          The next time I press my hand
on my lover, he would feel
          the gallop. The cavalry is here.
                    Every neigh & wild whip of hair.

JOSEPH SEES ME PAINTING MY THUMBS BLUE

(for my brother who almost happened)

Joseph sees me
painting my thumbs blue
like little cobalt sausages
jutting out from each palm.
My hands drip flowers
on each canvas, and it is his breath
that turns every petal,
curving outward just slightly at each end.

Sometimes my hand moves
my brush into a shape so perfect,
I know it cannot be of this earth.
And so, I think of my ancestors watching
over me, Joseph in front, leaning to guide
each stroke with his sure arm.

My brother, I never knew you,
and yet unfairly, you know everything
about me. Standing there in our father's
old shirt, I paint to talk to you.
I paint to talk with you
through my fingers, as if you lay
somewhere between the thin slips
of paint and my hand.

GOOD BLOOD

You have good blood, the nurse
informs me. Not too thin, and lots
of waxy fat cells, my very own
holly berries decking my veins.
Or does she mean my blood is warm—
not like the Atlantic at the end
of the year, cooling like soup

whenever a storm brews
the other side of the Earth?
Quite possibly, she means
it's the *color* that's just fine—
not purple, the pox
on my mother's plum tree—
not brown like weevils burying

themselves into acorns
on my street—but red, as in
pepper, wine, finch throats,
a ladybeetle's shell, the star
my father always points out
to me on my birthday,
two days before His.

THE ORIGINAL WILLIAM

with thanks to Kathy Fagan

Of course I called him *Billy*.
Number 56 on the field. *Bill* in the lunch line
in front of his friends. Smelled
of tap water and leather. Copied off me
in math. Pronounced my name
like a skin of plum caught
in his throat. Football hands.
My mother calls him *Bee-lee*,
as in, *Do you still talk*
to that Bee-lee? Very handsome,
that Bee-lee. The name presses
into the folds of my ear, gets stuck
in the tips of my glove—
sounds almost like believe.

MR. MUSTARD'S DANCE CLUB: LADIES' NIGHT

Seventeen, but we breezed right by the bouncers—
Me and Jill in tight tee-shirts and Levi's, flannel shirts

wrapped at our small waists. We danced together,
(never with boys) never drank, even when boys

offered to buy. Once, after I refused a beer, I heard
one say, "You know, them Asians can do

all those bending things." And I wondered *what*
bending things, what this had to do with taking

a sip from a cold bottle I didn't purchase. Still, we danced
to *Culture Club, Madonna, Men at Work, Banana-Rama*—

music we grew up with, heavy with keyboards
and drum machines. Our hairlines grew damp,

wisps of baby hair pulled loose from my ponytail.
Jill spied a water cooler by the phones and plucked

paper cones down for each of us to pour coolness,
to pour questions about people who bend.

BLUE TOPAZ

Of all the stones Marco Polo scattered on his bedside
table, he loved this one best. *Tapaz*, Sanskrit for fire,
hot star. He liked where it was found—in a cleft of rock,
a delicate fontanel, the earth around it full of worms
brimming blood. I own three: a heart pendant, a pair
of earrings, all presents from a boy I used to love.
December's stone of quiet light—sailors' girls wore
them strung with filigree above their ankles, miniature
oceans gathered at their chubby feet. Brazilians
believe it cures insomnia, asthma, even foggy vision.
Stone powers depend on the cycles of the moon. In my
trio, I sometimes see the sky that June day, the first tiny
box he ever gave a girl, the gem I used to roll between
my index finger and thumb, the small heat I felt there.

SMALL MURDERS

When Cleopatra received Antony on her cedarwood ship,
she made sure he would smell her in advance across the sea:
perfumed sails, nets sagging with rosehips and crocus
draped over her bed, her feet and hands rubbed in almond oil,
cinnamon, and henna. I knew I had you when you told me

you could not live without my scent, bought pink bottles of it,
creamy lotions, a tiny vial of *parfume*—one drop lasted all day.
They say Napoleon told Josephine not to bathe for two weeks
so he could savor her raw scent, but hardly any mention is ever
made of their love of violets. Her signature fragrance: a special blend

of these crushed purple blooms for wrist, cleavage, earlobe.
Some expected to discover a valuable painting inside
the locket around Napoleon's neck when he died, but found
a powder of violet petals from his wife's grave instead. And just
yesterday, a new boy leaned in close to whisper that he loved

the smell of my perfume, the one you handpicked years ago.
I could tell he wanted to kiss me, his breath heavy and slow
against my neck. My face lit blue from the movie screen—
I said nothing, only sat up and stared straight ahead. But
by evening's end, I let him have it: twenty-seven kisses

on my neck, twenty-seven small murders of you. And the count
is correct, I know—each sweet press one less number to weigh
heavy in the next boy's cupped hands. Your mark on me washed
away with each kiss. The last one so cold, so filled with mist
and tiny daggers, I already smelled blood on my hands.

BETELGEUSE

I've made a mess of it—I let him sweep his body
        over mine and I'm left to clear everything back
            into place: wax droplets hardening on my floor,
        water spilt on my bedside table, the smoke smell

on my ruffled pillows. Evidence enough.
        But before it was over, I took note
            of his shoulders, flecked with salty freckles
        and small dents from my fingernails. My favorite star

is Orion's shoulder: *Betelgeuse*—the one that hangs
        a bit higher than the other, red and brash, the one
            that ushers the hunter's sexy pose at night.
        Early Christians believed stars were rocks planted there

to keep people from climbing into Heaven
        on their own. I like to think of Orion—
            not hunting at the moment,
        but nudging fools like me out of the way, saying

not your turn, not like this. I ignore him, press on, until
        I come to that ruddy shoulder and find it's too big
            to even try to circle around. The way it pulses just a little
        makes me think of my own blood in my veins,

how it flows and kisses each muscle only
        as long as I stay put on this earth. And maybe he's right:
            scribbling notes on lovers' shoulders, necks, throats—
        is not the way. But I love the trying, not the mess, the rugs

and dust scattered. Only this sweet business of trying.

EATING DUST

Its dusty hairs tickle her *good mornings*
until the rinse and spit. Her toothbrush
combs her downy gums, erases the static

in her teeth. Fire ants eat just outside
her window. For days, she watches
each crystal of poison carried

back to their nest, every mandible
greedy and full. Before the grapefruit,
before the spoon, she tongues

the corners of her lips—her mouth
all crumb and salt, each cough
nobody's business but God's.

MOUTH STORIES

> "Its ridges, valleys, the corrugated roof, the fortress of teeth.
> There's a story trapped inside my mouth."
>
> —Jeanette Winterson, *Written on the Body*

sweet

Tight places between the molars,
the hollow under the tongue—
syrup-thick with desire, I find
my favorite place on your chest.
Your lips parted small while you sleep:
banana ice cream kiss.

sour

I leave your house before you
wake. The smash-smash of dead
leaves crumbles from the dark
corners of your frown. The ink
on yesterday's paper, cover
from the rain, drools down my cheek.

bitter

Like unripened pears for breakfast,
nausea rises into the back of my throat
when I think of your breath
warming someone else's thigh—
bottom lip cracked cold, I swallow
the last bit of blood.

salty

The skin between your shoulder
and neck is fresh on my tongue.
The first tear from your Bohemian
blue eye I lapped up by chance,
the second on purpose; I cannot rid
this taste from my mouth.

MOTORCYCLE

Whenever one pulled up beside me,
I'd look the other way, annoyed yet almost

scared, as if the rider would want to drag
down this stretch of hot pavement
against my sensible little brown car, else face

the wrath of his leather pants companion flipping
her hair extra for the wind. Crazy, I know—

but that's what I thought, till I met
a man who owns a Harley, likes
to plant geraniums, and doesn't

complain when he waits while I buy
another pair of shoes. Now I like to search

the metal curves of other bikes for tiny dents
and wonder where they have been, what state line
they'll cross next. The glitter in the paint. The sexy letters

that swirl into flame and spit. I like the sting
of the heated chrome against my calf, a hot bite

to wake me, hold his waist tighter. I don't wear
leather, fringe, thick boots. My cheek whipped
with my stray hair presses hard into his back

and the cars beside me now look so small,
their steering wheels too easy to hold—not like

this man, this blue bike, with all of this life.

LATE

He is too late for knives
and cutting boards wet with the juice
of fresh salmon, or maybe perch—
no time for cilantro to stick

under his nails. When he greets her *hello*
with his hand to her cheek, she'll know
exactly what will be on her plate. If he
didn't have to walk the dog, he'd be slicing

butter into a hot pan, striping cucumbers
and Walla Walla onions into a salad.
Instead, he pulls a thin box
from the freezer, zips a slice of air

into the apple crisp, the butterbar squash,
the meatloaf. The dial is set for five
and he steps away from the huzz
of the oven to check the street below.

He's late and he knows how she hates
to dash from car to theater, how
she'll lean away from him in the dark,
how he still needs time to buy his popcorn:

salt, no oil. The skin just under his earlobe
sweats lightly as he eats—skin that she likes
to tap with a finger, skin thin as a piece
of fresh vellum, just ripe for a calligraphy.

WHAT I LEARNED FROM THE INCREDIBLE HULK

When it comes to clothes, make
an allowance for the unexpected.
Be sure the spare in the trunk
of your station wagon with wood paneling

isn't in need of repair. A simple jean jacket
says *Hey, if you aren't trying to smuggle*
rare Incan coins through this peaceful
little town and kidnap the local orphan,

I can be one heck of a mellow kinda guy.
But no matter how angry a man gets, a smile
and a soft stroke on his bicep can work
wonders. I learned that male chests

also have nipples, warm and established—
green doesn't always mean envy.
It's the meadows full of clover
and chicory the Hulk seeks for rest, a return

to normal. And sometimes, a woman
gets to go with him, her tiny hands
correcting his rumpled hair, the cuts
in his hand. Green is the space between

water and sun, cover for a quiet man,
each rib shuttling drops of liquid light.

RED GHAZAL

I've noticed after a few sips of tea, the tip of her tongue, thin and red
with heat, quickens when she describes her cuts and bruises—deep violets and red.

The little girl I baby-sit, hair orange and wild, sits splayed and upside down
on a couch, insists her giant book of dinosaurs is the only one she'll ever read.

The night before I left him, I could not sleep, my eyes fixed on the freckles
of his shoulder, the glow of the clock, my chest heavy with dread.

Scientists say they'll force a rabbit to a bird, a jellyfish with a snake, even
though the pairs clearly do not mix. Some things are not meant to be bred.

I almost forgot the weight of a man sitting beside me in bed sheets crumpled
around our waists, both of us with magazines, laughing at the thing he just read.

He was so charming—pointed out planets, ghost galaxies, an ellipsis
of ants on the wall. And when he kissed me goodnight, my neck reddened.

I'm terrible at cards. Friends huddle in for Euchre, Hearts—beg me to play
with them. When it's obvious I can clearly win with a black card, I select a red.

I throw away my half-finished letters to him in my tiny pink wastebasket, but
my aim is no good. The floor is scattered with fire hazards, declarations unread.

ORIGIN OF THE MILKY WAY

after the painting with the same name by Tintoretto, 1564.

In this celestial boudoir, Hermes tries to force
Queen Hera's milk into baby Hercules at night.
But of course, as the way of these myths go,

there's an accident: her milk sprays instead
to an indigo sky, igniting into tiny flames
for the gods to pluck later, and arrange the way

a jeweler cunningly places his shiny stones
on velvet at just the perfect angle so the light
makes a woman say *Please dear, I want this one.*

I can't stop staring at the right-hand corner
of the painting, and I am reminded of the man
I miss, five hundred miles away. A peacock

and peahen sit nestled on a regal pillow—the male alert,
observing the fountain of light falling from the queen's breast.
A cherub flies above these birds, ready with a net

to kidnap Hera's prized possessions if she does not
comply. The birds should see what's coming,
but they don't: he is occupied, and the female turns away

as if she's tired already, or can't stand to see this brightness.
I secretly want them to be caught, bagged together if only
to have them look in the same direction again, bend their necks

close to plot their escape, vow a return to their willow tree—
the branches so lacy, so low, they touch the earth.

FABRIC

The last time you spun silk
into my thighs,   I forgot to take
note of the song on the radio,
        all I remember is a dog barking
in the alley, a shake of chains—

        and then   the glow of streetlights.
Now I think perhaps it was not silk,
but *toile de jouy*, a rougher fabric, pale twill
with French blue designs of country life, scenes lifted
        from a children's book or play:

                there is a merry man playing a flute
        above my ankle, a blue cat following his every step.
Across my hips   I feel the breeze
        from a cottage window, some hot pastry
                cooling on the sill. I can just imagine

you setting your little workers to task—
a small factory   for waffled cloth and pastel damasks.
Inside, the light bulbs remain on and on.   As long as
                we stayed there we kept
        everything bright from breaking.

SPICES

coloring

If your man doesn't know cumin
from cardamom, it's time to let him go.
But if he discovers a wetted paintbrush dipped
into turmeric makes a soft yellow line
on your back, spells something like *You*
are my sun—then keep him and hold on tight.
I like a cupboard packed with jam jars rubbed clean,
full of the sand from fantasy beaches of me
and my man and a paintbrush I conjured up
just last night—a cupboard where the difference in reds
means danger or victory for my pot of stew.

fragrance

And what about cloves pierced
into a fat orange, strung up with ribbon
at Christmas? Who came up with that,
and what kind of twisted need did they have
for the occasional prick of spikes under
nails? Once, when we were leaving
Bombay Palace, my father spooned
caraway and licorice bits into my palm
from the jade bowl on the counter and said,
"This will clean your breath." The owner
twitched his mustache, and nodded.

heat

Pepper is the obvious choice, in its powder form,
I mean—but there's something about the crush
of peppercorns into a salad, over pasta, the twist
and flex of wrist that sends men back for more.
But if you really want to impress, try chili flaked fresh

under a rolling pin and wax paper. Make sure he sees
you doing this labor of love—act as if you do this
at every meal, that this is how it would be every day
if he desired. And after dinner, float some
in his tea, slip some into his slice of cake.
Be careful for the warmth of his mouth.

ARE YOU MAKING DUMB CAKE?
British Isles

Shhhh. I need complete silence. Turn off the radio,
take off your clickety shoes. Don't even *think*
of bringing that baby into the kitchen. This cake

needs Quiet to predict who you will marry.
Twirl the egg like a top on the counter before
you break it. I need three more whisked (so rich
so creamy) in this silver bowl. Complete. Silence.

Push your thumb into each shell, pour oil into the heap
of flour slowly, least you make even a tiny, tinny sound—
like a cold creek sliding over shale. Prick your initials

in the batter to make a boggy cloud appear—
your future love's face—hovering in your oven.
If you don't like who you see, eat your sorrow
in spongy forkfuls and brush the crumbs

from the corners of your very dry mouth. I know
how it is to want to taste a neat husband, savor
your future house, lick the windows clean.

UNDER WATER, BEHIND GLASS

At the National Aquarium in Washington D.C.,
I wander around the basement maze of animals

(under water, behind glass) with the man
who was my first love. All the green-gray light,

the pink glow of the anemone, the white-tipped spikes
of the lion fish—make his skin a color I can't

even name. It's been five years but still I know
the brush of his coat behind me, the cup

of his hand as we cross the street, his smell like trees.
We are silent most of the time, except for a few tugs

and nudges to *look at this one! Check out these eyes!*
Children with starfish-shaped lollipops drool

at the railing, smudge their wet noses on the tanks
of sea snakes and a lone octopus peeping back

at them from behind a boulder, one tentacle
unfurled as if asking for a lick. At the lobster exhibit

we read the light-up panels: "Lobsters line up
single file as far as the eye can see and walk

hundreds of feet to find their one mate." And I know
what he is thinking. It is what I am thinking:

if all this time and space has been *our* walk, our journey
to fit again into the last voices we hear at night.

But this is too easy. Right now, we are too much
in wonder—the next series of tanks shows us how

one of the Southern flounder's eyes eventually migrates
to the other side of its flat head, till one side holds

both eyes, like a cartoon fish—the other side struck
blind to all of the wild diatoms in full bloom.

MY NAME

At four, I was ready: fat pencil and paper, lined
the way I like it best—two strong sky blue lines
with a dotted line in between the two, a soft ceiling
for the tops of lower case letters to brush up against.

In New Guinea, to identify a person's family, you ask,
What is the name of your canoe? My seventh grade
social studies teacher made up a dance to help him
remember how to pronounce my name—he'd break it

into sharp syllables, shake his corduroyed hips
at roll call, his bulge of keys rattling in time.
I don't remember who first shortened it to Nez,
but I loved the zip of it, the sport and short of it,

until the day I learned Nez means *nose* in French.
Translation: beloved nose. My father tells me part
of our name comes from a flower from the South Indian
coast. I wonder what it smells like, what fragrance

I always have dabbed at my neck. Scientists say some flowers
don't have a scent, but they *do*—even if it's hints of sweat
from blooms too long without drink or the promise
of honey from the scratchings of a thin bee leg, feathered

with loosestrife and sage. I wonder if I've ever smelled
our flower, if the smell ever wafted clear across the ocean.
I would swim out to meet it, brush the salt and bits
of pink shell away, apologize for the messiness of my hair.

ACKNOWLEDGMENTS

Grateful acknowledgment to the editors of the following magazines in which these poems first appeared, some in earlier versions:

Atlanta Review, "The Rolling Saint."
Bellingham Review, "Blue Topaz," "*Aanabhrandhanmar* Means Mad About Elephants."
Beloit Poetry Journal, "Wrap," "Ooty Lake."
Chelsea, "Speak," "Arachne," "One Bite."
Chiron Review, "Our Time."
Crab Orchard Review, "Mr. Mustard's Dance Club: Ladies Night."
The Emrys Journal, "The Original William."
The Evansville Review, "Cheese Curds, The First Time."
Green Hills Literary Lantern, "Cocoa Beach, Off-Season."
The Kerf, "Crow Joy."
The MacGuffin, "Red Ghazal."
The Massachusetts Review, "Peacocks," "Winter Games."
Mid-American Review, "What I Learned From the Incredible Hulk," "Gulabjamoon Jar."
Nimrod: International Journal of Poetry and Fiction, "Spices."
North American Review, "Swear Words."
Northwest Florida Review, "Confusions," Fabric," "Origin of the Milky Way."
The Oregon Review, "Meditation on Flannel."
Poetry Northwest, "The Bonsai Master's Daughter Breaks Her Silence," "The Woman Who Turned Down a Date with a Cherry Farmer," "Why I Am Not Afraid of King Cobras," "Under Water, Behind Glass."
Prairie Schooner, "Hell Pig," "Suddenly As Anything."
Ratapallax, "Coco Cay."
River Styx, "Telling the Bees."
Shenandoah, "Small Murders."
Snowy Egret Journal, "The Alligator."
Southern Indiana Review, "Falling Thirds."
The Southern Review, "Making Gyotaku."
Sunstone, "Table Manners."
Spoon River Poetry Review, "Firsts," "Stealing Song."
Whirligig, "Late."

*

Special thanks to Ken Denberg and the Snail's Pace Press,
who published my chapbook, *Fishbone*, winner of the Snail's Pace Press Prize,
in which some of these poems also appear.

***

"Lewis and Clark Disagree" appear in *Sad Little Breathings and Other Acts of Ventriloquism*, PublishingOnline Press. ed. Heather McHugh; "Fishbone," "Ooty Lake," and "One Bite," appear in *BABAYLAN: An Anthology of Filipina Poetry and Prose*, Aunt Lute Press. eds. Eileen Tabios and Nick Carbo; "Hell Pig," and "Swear Words" appear in *Humor Me: An Anthology of Humor by Writers of Color*, University of Iowa Press. ed. John McNally; "Swear

Words," appears in *Filipino Writers in the Diaspora*, Anvil Publishing. ed. Luisa A. Igloria; "Coco Cay," appears in *Pinoy Poetics: An Anthology of Filipino Poets and Poetry*, Meritage Press. ed. Eileen Tabios. "The Woman Who Turned Down a Date with a Cherry Farmer," "Mouth Stories," "Red Ghazal," "Fishbone," and "What I Learned From the Incredible Hulk," appear in *Asian American Poetry—The Next Generation*. ed. Victoria Chang; "In Praise of Colophons," "Betelgeuse," and "Fruit Cocktail Tree," appear in (**www.canwehaveourballback.com**); "Wrap" was featured on Poetry Daily's website (**www.poems.com**); "Small Murders," was featured on Verse Daily's website (**www.versedaily.org**).

***

"Under Water, Behind Glass," "Why I am Not Afraid of King Cobras," and "The Woman Who Turned Down a Date with a Cherry Farmer," received the 2002 Richard Hugo Prize from *Poetry Northwest*.
"Speak" was selected for *Beacon Best of 2000: Great Writing by Women and Men of All Colors and Cultures*, Beacon Press. ed. Edwidge Danticat.
"Mouth Stories" was the winner of the 1999 *Atlantic Monthly's* Student Writer Contest.
"Cocoa Beach, Off-Season" was nominated for a Pushcart Prize.
"Gulabjamoon Jar" was an Editor's Choice in the *Mid-American Review's* Fineline Competition.

***

I've been blessed to have such good people supporting me: The folks at Ohio State University, especially David Citino for his superhuman thoughtfulness and energy to nudge me along every step of the way, Michael Lohre—the first reader of many of these poems, editing with the keenest of eye and ear—and for his unconditional faith in me, Bill Roorbach, Sara Sutherland, Americ McCullagh, Ron Degenfelder, Debra Whitman, Jennifer Vanderbes, Sharon Stephenson, Mark Steinwachs, Toi Derricote, Lynn Emanuel, Carol Houck-Smith, Eileen Tabios, Nick Carbo, and Denise Duhamel. A very special thanks to Ron Wallace, Jesse Lee Kercheval, Diane Middlebrook, my fellow fellows, and the Wisconsin Institute of Creative Writing for the funding, time, and lovely surroundings to finish this project. Muchas gracias to my colleagues at SUNY-Fredonia for their encouragement, my students past and present, and to Nathan Smith for his advice and laughter. I'm deeply grateful to Gregory Orr for selecting this book, and especially to Jeffrey Levine and everyone at Tupelo Press. And finally, to JoAnn—all my adoration. You are my pearl.